Decluttering Your Home

8 Simple Everyday Minimalism Techniques to Declutter Your Home & Mind - With Meditations for Spirituality, Mindfulness, Healthy Habits and Self Affirmations

By

Lauren Marshall

© Copyright 2018

Lauren Marshall - All rights reserved.

The following eBook is reproduced below with the goal of providing information that is as accurate and reliable as possible. Regardless, purchasing this eBook can be seen as consent to the fact that both the publisher and the author of this book are in no way experts on the topics discussed within and that any recommendations or suggestions that are made herein are for entertainment purposes only. Professionals should be consulted as needed prior to undertaking any of the action endorsed herein.

This declaration is deemed fair and valid by both the American Bar Association and the Committee of Publishers Association and is legally binding throughout the United States.

Furthermore, the transmission, duplication or reproduction of any of the following work including specific information will be considered an illegal act irrespective of if it is done electronically or in print. This extends to creating a secondary or tertiary copy of the work or a recorded copy and is only allowed with express written consent from the Publisher. All additional right reserved.

The information in the following pages is broadly considered to be a truthful and accurate account of facts and as such any inattention, use or misuse of the information in question by the reader will render any resulting actions solely under their purview. There are no scenarios in which the publisher or the original author of this work can be in any fashion deemed liable for any hardship or damages that may befall them after undertaking information described herein.

Additionally, the information in the following pages is intended only for informational purposes and should thus be thought of as universal. As befitting its nature, it is presented without assurance regarding its prolonged validity or interim quality. Trademarks that are mentioned are done without written consent and can in no way be considered an endorsement from the trademark holder.

Medical Disclaimer

This book is not intended as a substitute for the medical advice of physicians. The reader should regularly consult a physician in matters relating to his/her health and particularly with respect to any symptoms that may require diagnosis or medical attention. Any recommendations given in this book are not a substitute for medical advice.

Contents

Introduction 6

Chapter One: The Importance of Decluttering and Minimalism 11

    Why Do We Accumulate Clutter? 13

    How Does Clutter Affect Our Health? 17

Chapter Two: Freeing Yourself from Clutter 26

Chapter Three: The Importance of Mindfulness and Meditation 35

    The Three Types of Meditation – And Which One is Right for You 40

    Hidden Benefits of Meditation You Never Knew About 43

    How to meditate, even if you've never done it before in your life 49

Chapter Four: 8 Exercises for Everyday Mindfulness You Can Do at Home...with no extra cost 57

Introduction

For most of us, living with clutter is simply a way of life. Accumulating possessions is something that we do without giving it much thought. Think about the last time you moved. How many boxes and crates and bags of things did you discover while you were packing that you forgot you even had? How much of this stuff did you choose to keep, for one reason or another, even though you had just rediscovered you had it in the first place? How many times did you look at an object or piece of clothing and decided that you simply couldn't bear to part with it, even though you hadn't worn, used or even acknowledged that it existed in years? Simply put, as we go through life, we accumulate clutter. As the late comedian George Carlin famously quoted in his standup routine, "a house is just a place to keep your stuff while you go out and get more stuff." While this may seem oversimplified, there is a great deal of wisdom in that comical assertation.

Even those of us who like to consider ourselves neat, orderly and organized are not exempt from this tendency. We just conceal it better. Think about it. Everyday, we wake up and go out to do whatever it is that we do in the world. For some of us, this means going to work, while for others, it means raising children, upkeeping a home, attending classes or any other number of activities. Each and every day, no matter what we do, most of us are bound to collect at least one piece of clutter, if not much more than that. At least one piece of paper or magazine will make its way on to the coffee table or kitchen island, never to be glanced at again. Maybe we will find some object in the store that appeals to us for one reason or another, only to purchase it, bring it home, and then promptly forget about it, leaving it to gather dust on the shelf. There might be a tremendous sale at our favorite store, where we will go and purchase things that we kind of like simply because it's a good deal. We might bring home a bag of clothes that aren't really our style and not quite our size, but we simply had to buy them, because it was such a good deal and someone someday might make use of them.

How many of us have a closet or two crammed full of clothes, books and toys that our children haven't touched in over ten years? How many kitchens have shelves lined with dishes that haven't been used since the latest set was purchased, or a cabinet containing Tupperware and plastic containers that are never actually used to store food? How many of us have homes that contain a junk drawer or two, where we toss all of the odds and ends we pick up throughout the day? How many of our bathroom cabinets are lined with half-used personal hygiene products and/or cosmetics we used once or twice and didn't really like, but for some reason, can't bring ourselves to throw it in the trash? Even after we no longer have a need for the possessions we have accumulated, we tend to stubbornly hold on to them.

There are a number of reasons for our refusal to let go. Maybe we don't want to get rid of any piece of artwork our children ever painted or any article of clothing they ever wore when they were a baby simply because we are trying to hold onto the child that they once were. Maybe we don't want to throw away the brochures, maps and travel guides from our latest vacation because we somehow think that if we do so, we might not remember the experience as well. Maybe we keep notes from our high school friends and movie ticket/concert stubs and other random memorabilia with the vague idea of creating a scrapbook someday.

While the urge to collect clutter is certainly common, it is also ultimately detrimental to our mental and even physical well-being. The constant accumulation of possessions can make the entire ambiance of our home chaotic and unorganized, rather than the welcome respite from the outside world that it is intended to be. Likewise, holding onto too much stuff can actually harm you physically, as it creates a breeding ground for dust and mold, along with creating potential fall hazards and blocking routes of escape in case of an emergency.

The aim of this book is to help the reader understand how decluttering and minimalism can greatly improve your life. In the following pages, we will farther explore the connection between clutter and the effect it has on the mind and bod. We will also explain how ridding yourself of clutter and unnecessary possessions helps to provide a liberating effect, and also improves concentration and promotes relaxation. The first part of this book delves into the connection between your physical surroundings and your state of mind/being. It explains the reasons behind why we constantly accumulate clutter, and introduces the concepts of decluttering and minimalism. We will learn practical ways to remove clutter from our home to create an environment that promotes serenity and contentment. The second part of the book introduces the concept of mindfulness, and how it is related to eliminating clutter. Here, we will learn about meditation and different techniques that we can use throughout the day in any situation to help alleviate stress and anxiety.

Chapter One: The Importance of Decluttering and Minimalism

In 2014, Japanese author Marie Kondo released her book titled <u>The Life-Changing Magic of Tidying Up: The Japanese Art of Decluttering and Organization.</u> Widely heralded as the decluttering Bible, her book has since gone on to be a New York Times Bestseller, with over seven million copies sold worldwide and having been translated into over thirty different languages! Kondo's popularity doesn't stop there, however! She has a waiting list for personally consulting clients that wraps around the block, as well as bearing the title of being one of Time Magazine's 100 most influential people. This book is widely based around the Japanese concept of the value behind decluttering and minimalism.

Simply put, decluttering refers to the process of getting rid of all of our unnecessary possessions. Minimalism is about achieving freedom through simplicity. In today's consumer culture, it is very easy to become caught up in the game of accumulating possessions. From a very young age, most of us are taught that in order to be successful and happy, we must acquire a car, a house, and then fill said house with all kinds of possessions. In much of the world, the possessions we have directly reflect our status, thus we accumulate as much as we can as fast as we can, just so that everyone knows how important we are. Even when these possessions are no longer useful, we loathe to part with them, just in case we may somehow find a use for them again someday. Minimalism teaches us that by no longer allowing our possessions to define our worth, we are able to achieve greater freedom and liberate our minds from thinking we must cling to every possession we have ever had. Instead of focusing upon the material things surrounding us, minimalism places emphasis on finding happiness via exploring life, interacting with loved ones and most of all, by focusing upon creating a state of mind that makes you happy.

Why Do We Accumulate Clutter?

Generally speaking, there are three major reasons why people tend to accumulate and hang onto clutter. These are related to feelings of nostalgia, perceptions of future utility and appreciation for beauty and quality.

Let's tackle the big one first. Nostalgia is hands-down the most common reason people resist against decluttering. Our hearts and heads often have very different priorities, and nowhere is this discrepancy more apparent than in the concept of decluttering your home and life. Of course, we still have the lock of hair from our daughter's first haircut hidden away, along with the first tooth she ever lost and the birthday candle from her first cake. Same goes with an article of clothing, handwritten note or other possession that was once the property of a loved one who is now deceased. Even though we may never actually take these keepsakes out and look at or appreciate them, we get a strange sense of comfort just knowing that we have them. As is the case with a huge number of our possessions that have become clutter, we have an emotional attachment to these objects. They are keepsakes of a person or moment in time that we wish to remember and keep with us forever. On some sort of level, in our heads we fear that if we were to get rid of these things, we will somehow lose our connection with the person it represents to us. Throwing away these keepsakes equates to throwing away precious memories, and this is something that we naturally resist against. In almost every instance, nostalgic clutter is by far the easiest to accumulate and the hardest to let go of.

Another reason why we tend to hang onto clutter is out of the pervasive belief that perhaps, someday, we may have a need for every object we have ever acquired. Maybe you haven't lived in an area where snow accumulation is a viable possibility for over two years, yet you still refuse to part with the down jacket and winter boots stashed away in the closet, just in case a rogue blizzard was to suddenly hit town. Even if our own children haven't played with the board games and stuffed animals tucked away in the attic for over a decade, we hold onto it, just in case our younger sibling or cousin decides to have a baby one day, and might want to make use of it. College textbooks sit on the bookcase, accumulating dust, yet we spent good money on those books, and you never know, someday there might be a need for a refresher course in calculus. As humans, we have a natural tendency to want to be prepared for every situation. We cling to the possessions we acquire, storing them away in attics, basements and closets with the idea that they are there waiting for us if the need for them ever arises. Most of us were also raised with the idea that wastefulness is bad. Therefore, we feel that if we throw away the things that we or someone else paid good money for, we are wasting that money.

Finally, we sometimes accumulate and hold onto clutter for aesthetic reasons. While the stained glass lamp our sister-in-law bought us for a Christmas present four years ago may not be our style, the sheer beauty of the lamp makes us feel as though we must put it on display and keep it in our homes. The sheet set we bought because it was such a good deal may never actually be used on the bed, but we can't bear to part with it, because they felt so soft in the store and we know they are of a high quality. For those of us who collect things, this is an area where hanging onto something purely because of its visual appeal can cause clutter to become out of control. Even if we know we do not need more porcelain dolls, model airplanes, paintings or whatever it is we collect, we will continue to purchase and hoard these things out of habit, and because we know that a new addition will look so pretty next to all of its counterparts.

One of the first steps in deciding to declutter your home is to identify which of these three categories the majority of your clutter falls into. Once you have a true understanding as to why you accumulate clutter, you will be in a better position to honestly evaluate your attachment to your possessions. For instance, for those of us who collect clutter for nostalgic reasons, we must begin with a psychological shift that allows us to accept that letting go of objects does not mean we are letting go of memories or our loved ones.

How Does Clutter Affect Our Health?

Even though we may think that the objects which make up the clutter we accumulate brings us comfort, status and security, multiple studies have shown that keeping clutter around can actually have some very serious side effects on both the mind and the body. As humans, we are conditioned to want to hold on to everything we have, yet clinging to our possessions can cause us serious harm. Let's examine some of the ways that clutter can adversely affect us.

Clutter can contribute to higher stress levels

A recent study conducted at the University of Los Angeles found that having clutter lying around the home or office can significantly increase stress levels, particularly in women. Everything from dirty dishes in the sink to an ever-mounting stack of laundry to wash, fold and dry to an explosion of papers strewn across the desk can make it very difficult for us to truly relax when we come home at night. Likewise, a work space that is constantly cluttered markedly contributes to a sense of stress and discontentment.

The presence of clutter raises the stress hormone cortisol in our brains. This, coupled with the excessive visual stimulation that accompanies a cluttered environment can cause us to feel anxious, irritable and perpetually on edge. Every time we walk into a room, we are reminded of all the work and cleaning that needs to be done. If we want to have friends over for dinner and drinks, preparing for what should be a happy event becomes extremely stressful as we race around the home to make it look clean and organized.

Clutter can cost you money

Paper is an enormous source of clutter, even in today's paperless, email-driven society. Most of

Decluttering Your Home

us have at least one area in our homes that acts as a landing zone for every piece of paper that comes through the door, whether it be junk mail, coupons, fliers, renewal notices, bills, etc. When all of these papers are kept in disorganized piles rather than being neatly filed and systematically thrown away, it is very easy to lose track of important financial documents. We might forget to pay our cable bill until we start getting phone calls because the actual bill has been buried under a mountain of other papers since it first arrived in the mail three weeks ago. We might have to pay a ticket because our car has been unregistered for over a week, simply because the renewal form got lost in the chaos and was forgotten.

It is not only misplacing or losing things in the clutter that can have an impact on our finances. When we have so many possessions laying around in multiple places, it can be very difficult to know exactly what we actually have. Take for example the simple activity of hanging up a few pictures in the family room. You know that somewhere in the house, you have nails and a hammer, but after spending half an hour searching, still can't seem to locate either one. You go to the hardware store, buy the tools you need, and come home to hang the pictures. The hammer and unused nails promptly disappear into the void of clutter in the basement, meeting the same fate as their predecessors. Say that a week later, you need to hang another picture. Again, you can't locate the tools you need, so you go out and buy them *again*. In a home without clutter, you would know exactly where to look. There wouldn't be a waste of time hunting things down, as the tools would be placed back in the same location each time immediately after being used.

Clutter decreases focus and lowers levels of concentration

Have you ever woken up with a clear list of things you'd like to accomplish that morning? Say that your goal is to go for an early jog and cook yourself a healthy, hot breakfast before jumping in the shower and sprucing up a little before you have to leave for work. You've planned it out so you'll be ahead of the traffic, with fifteen minutes to settle in and get comfortable before your first meeting. You feel ready to take on the day as you hop out of bed. It takes you a minute to find your shoes (they were under the bed), and while you're tying them on before headed out the door, you realize that the roll of plastic wrap is still sitting on the kitchen counter from the night before. You pause for a moment and walk over to put it away, and noticing that there are a few glasses and plates in the sink, stop again to rinse them and load the dishwasher. The rubber bone you trip over in the front hallway reminds you to stop and fill dishes with food and change water bowls, and the shirt hanging over the back of a chair must go into the wash before you can begin the day. You finally make it out the door, and have a brief reprieve of relaxation while jogging, but as soon as you get home and check the time, you realize that your way behind schedule. You want to cook something for breakfast, but the refrigerator is in such a state of disarray you can't find the ingredients you need for anything besides coffee and cold cereal. On your way to the shower, you pause to collect a few of the kid's toys and put them back in their proper place. By the time you actually get yourself in the shower, you have just enough time to put together a single outfit from your overflowing closet and jump in the car, only to barely arrive on time.

The presence of clutter distracts us from what we are trying to do. By ultimately eliminating the cutter we have in our everyday surroundings, we eliminate the majority of the distractions we face every day. Without a multitude of unfinished tasks staring us in the face at each moment, we are able to quickly accomplish exactly what we set out to do.

Clutter can make it hard to breathe

The more objects we have, the more we open the door to those things accumulating dust or even growing mold. The presence of mold or dust in the environment can have significant negative effects upon the respiratory system. Those who live with clutter run the risk of compromising their immune system, leading to an increase in everything from the common cold to influenza and even pneumonia. People with an already compromised respiratory tract, such as those who suffer from asthma, COPD or allergies are particularly susceptible to the detrimental potential side effects of a cluttered environment.

Clutter can literally cost you your life

Most of us have seen television shows which showcase individuals who have taken accumulating clutter to the extreme form of hoarding. In some of these cases, people find it virtually impossible to part with anything, thus, they end up living in a home that has every surface covered with papers, boxes and all other kinds of possessions. You cannot move easily through the hallways. You cannot access or open the windows and doors. And yet, what the majority of people do not realize is that we don't have to go to the extreme of hoarding for our clutter to present a serious potential issue to our personal safety. Large stacks of paper or other flammable materials present a definite fire hazard. The fall hazard presented by disorganization is very real as well, as is the possibility for potential emergency exits being compromised in the moment they are needed the most.

Clutter can compromise your sense of well-being

The connection between the mind and body is well documented, and very real. If something negatively impacts our brains and emotions, that same thing has the power to likewise manifest negatively in the body. When we live in a home with clutter, our personal lives feel more cluttered and chaotic as well. When our workspace is cluttered, we often find that we have a hard time focusing and moving forward at work. According to the principles of Feng Shui, a Chinese practice that stresses the harmonization of energetic forces throughout the home, clutter is nothing more than wasted space that constantly sucks away and blocks energy. Once the clutter is removed, beneficial energies have the opportunity to move freely, which opens the gateways for contentment and satisfaction.

Chapter Two: Freeing Yourself from Clutter

Perhaps today is the day that you decide to make a change. Making the decision to be an active participant in the decluttering process is certainly first and arguably the hardest step. The thought of methodically sorting through all of our possessions and ruthlessly tossing aside all but the most functional/favorite initially seems cold, unfeeling and even unnatural. We may feel an initial moment of panic, worried that we will be parting from things that we carry attachment to, for whatever reason. And yet, as intimidating as the process may seem at first, the vast majority of people who choose to declutter their homes experience higher levels of happiness and contentment as a result. Some people delight in the fact that everything in their home now serves a purpose or brings happiness, while others appreciate the more practical aspects of decluttering, meaning the home is far easier to keep clean and organized.

If you have decided that you are interested in decluttering, it is important to go about the process the right way. It can appear to be very overwhelming, or even impossible at first. Below is a list of steps that can help you prioritize your possessions and mindfully restore order and control to your life.

Step One: Set realistic expectations

Unless you are going to immerse yourself one hundred percent in a strict minimalistic lifestyle, there will never be zero clutter. This is a simple fact of life and one that needs to be accepted. If you are raising young children, it is virtually impossible to immediately put everything back in its place every time. And you certainly don't want to waste the magic and wonder of their younger years by obsessively worrying about messes. In some instances, we must acknowledge that we can only do the best we can in terms of keeping clutter at bay.

Step Two: Take a deep breath

Yes, the initial though of decluttering your home is scary. Even though you know you don't need all the stuff taking up space in your closets and basement and attic, on some sort of primal, emotional level, our hearts still skip a beat at the thought of parting with it. This is when it is particularly important to understand the reasoning behind we accumulate and hold onto clutter. Once we understand the motivations behind a behavior, it is much easier to look at it in a rational, realistic manner rather than allowing it to mindlessly control our behavior.

Step Three: Get everyone on board

Even if you are wholeheartedly dedicated to decluttering your home, the process is not going to work if your spouse comes home every night with an armload of junk mail and leaves his shoes in the middle of the kitchen floor. If your roommate is bringing things into the apartment as fast as you can mindfully move them out, you are fighting a loosing battle. In order for the decluttering process to truly work, everyone in the household must be on board and on the same page.

Step Four: Take it one room or category at a time

The worst thing you can do in the beginning stages of the decluttering process is to self-sabotage. If you wake up one morning and decide that you are going to somehow declutter your entire home by sundown, you are almost certainly setting yourself up for failure. Odds are, you have been in your home for at least some period of time, and in keeping with human nature, you have accumulated possessions accordingly. Rather than putting pressure on yourself to do too much too fast, break the process down into small, manageable chunks.

Set yourself a goal each day, and accomplish it. Some people like to work one room at a time, meaning one day they tackle the clutter in the bedroom and another day, tackle it in the kitchen. Other people prefer to declutter their homes by category. This means one day, you might make the choice to go through and declutter your books and magazines, while another day, you might focus on clothing or children's toys.

Step Five: Touch, ask, acknowledge and decide

Say that it is your first day of the decluttering process, and you are taking on your first room or category. First and foremost, keep in mind that decluttering is supposed to be a cathartic, empowering activity rather than something that is traumatic or stress-inducing. The idea is to make the purging process an enjoyable, mindful moment rather than increasing anxiety. So, don't be in a hurry, and don't put too much pressure on yourself. Go into the task with an open yet firm mindset. As you go through the first room or category, let your own inner voice be the guide for what you should keep and what you should let go. One of the best ways to do this is through first physically touching and examining the object. Use all of your senses, if you can. Feel its texture in your hands, take in each detail with your eyes and breathe in its aroma. Once you have thoroughly examined the object in your hands, take a moment, and honestly ask yourself if whether or not that particular object brings you joy or serves an active purpose in your life. If the answer is yes, keep it in a place of honor and enjoy its presence daily. If the answer is no, put it aside. If you truly can't remember the last time you wore that beautiful red dress you bought on vacation years ago, it is probably time to let it go. Yes, you may have paid a lot of money for it, and yes, it reminds you of a wonderful point in time, but the reality is, it doesn't do much besides hang in your closet anymore.

This does not mean that you are expected to coldly toss your once beloved possessions in the trash as soon as you've decided you no longer need them. Giving thanks is an important part in the decluttering process. Acknowledge the role that this particular possession has played in your life, and the place it holds in your heart. It is certain that some things will carry too much sentimental, practical, material or aesthetic value to part with, but those things should be few and far between. Keeping one or two of your most treasured artifacts from your children's baby days is fine, but an entire box? Probably not. This is where you must be ruthless, and decide whether or not you truly need the object you have in your hands. If the answer is not an immediate yes, joyfully release the object and let it go, confident in the knowledge that someone else may have an actual need for it.

Step Six: Create a maintenance plan

The tendency to accumulate clutter is insidious. Once you have gone through the decluttering process, it is important to keep your guard up and formulate a plan to ensure the continued organization and serenity of your home. One of the simplest yet most commonly overlooked ways to keep clutter at bay is to get into the practice of immediately putting things back where they belong. Instead of walking through the door at night and tossing your keys on the counter and your jacket on the back of the couch, take the extra time to hang everything up where it belongs. It seems such an insignificant step, but having everything in its place goes an unbelievably long way to creating an orderly, serene environment.

Another major way to prevent clutter from piling up is to come up with a system. Instead of allowing papers to pile up, get in the habit of going through the mail and other papers each and every day. Promptly throw out anything you do not have a need for, such as junk mail. For the things you may want temporarily, such as a magazine or grocery flier, it is ok to hold onto it just long enough to read it, after which, it needs to be sent on its way. For the few and far between papers you do actually need to keep, such as bills and important documents, file these neatly away in a spot that allows you quick access without constantly being in your line of vision.

The bottom line is that you need to come up with a maintenance plan for minimizing clutter that works for you. Some people like to live by the rule of one-in, one-out. This means that if you make the choice to bring something new into the house, such as an article of clothing or book, you must balance the new possession's presence by getting rid of something else. Other people strongly benefit from picking a set date, be it once a week or month to dedicate entirely to walking through each room in the home and removing any possessions which are no longer necessary. As long as it yields the results you want, there is no truly right or wrong way to keep clutter accumulation at bay.

Chapter Three: The Importance of Mindfulness and Meditation

What is Mindfulness?

Simply put, to be mindful means to live in the moment. It means being aware of your surroundings and taking in what is going on around you with all of your senses, and not allowing yourself to be sidetracked by anxiety or other emotions. While this may seem simple, remaining mindful in today's hectic world is a great challenge indeed. When we are in a mindful state, we are able to objectively and fully observe what is going on around us. Likewise, we are then able to appreciate our surroundings to their fullest extent, and can respond to people and situations with objectivity and wisdom rather than blind emotion or instinct alone. To be mindful means that we are fully present and engaged in the moment we are experiencing. We only take in what is happening now, rather than allowing the moment to be overshadowed by demons from the past or insecurities about the future.

There are two basic tenants of mindfulness – staying in the moment and reserving judgment,

Staying in the moment means exactly what is sounds like. Particularly if we are a naturally a little high strung, the concept of being present in the moment and not worrying about the past or future can be a little intimidating. Yes, we all can agree that it would be fantastic to be able to only focus upon what is happening immediately in front of us, but there are many different variables, such as children playing in the next room, pets scampering about outside or any other number of things that make it very difficult to keep our mind in the present moment. This is where it is important to have a true understanding as to what it really means to be fully present in the moment, and mindful. Mindfulness does not ask us to forget about our responsibilities and obligations. It is not a simple philosophy of out of sight, out of mind.

Instead of worrying about what could possibly be wrong and fretting that we do not have enough, mindfulness teaches us the value of appreciating what we already have. When we stop comparing our lives and possessions to others and learn to see the value of the things already surrounding us, we find it much easier to want to be present in the moment. Instead of worrying that we will not have enough resources to fend of potential disaster someday, we are able to rest assured that we have all we need for now, and can take contentment in knowing that that is enough in and of itself.

The second major aspect of achieving mindfulness is reserving judgment. Instead of instantly judging a person or situation as good or bad, we instead take the time to consider the possibility that everything happens for a reason. For example, if we fail to achieve a certain goal, such as landing a particular job, getting into a certain college or winning the affections of a certain someone, we may be tempted to fall into a state of despair, beating ourselves up over what we perceive as a failed result. And yet if we to are consider the same problem from a standpoint of mindfulness, we realize that we have not failed. When we reserve judgment and focus upon living in the present moment, it is much easier to accept that each perceived failure conceals some sort of hidden lesson. Yes, the job you went after may have gone to someone else. Yes, the man or woman you shamelessly wooed last weekend may be stepping out without someone else the next day. The test you prepared so meticulously for might have included questions that your notes couldn't groom you for.

Does this mean that you failed? Absolutely not. This is where reserving judgment comes into play. Do not judge your recent breakup as being good or bad, instead simply accept it as something that happened, acknowledge and honor it, and then move on. It does us absolutely no good to dwell upon the guilt and/or regret associated with the past, just as it is equally useless to obsess and worry over the future. At each and every point in your life, you are perceiving what is happening in the present. To pay attention to anything else distracts from the concept of mindfulness.

Being mindful is a mental state that may require some form of practicing to achieve. Most likely, we have grown up in a consumer culture, and have therefore been taught that our possessions make up our status and reflect who we are. We are also taught that we must constantly be vigilant of downplaying our past and grooming our future to ensure the best life possible. We think that we must judge, compete against and outshine others in order for our own worth to be evident. When we make the choice to move towards choosing mindfulness, we willingly and joyfully let go of every regret from our past along with any anxiety regarding our future. Instead, we focus upon making the absolute best out of every moment as it presents itself to us.

There are a number of different ways to encourage a state of mindfulness. These include participation in daily prayers, getting into the habit of morning affirmations and/or statements of gratitude as well as an increase in physical activity, such as taking up yoga, jogging or any other sport that helps you focus your energy. Yet multiple studies suggest that one of the quickest ways to make mindfulness an every day part of life is through regular participation in some sort of meditative process.

The Three Types of Meditation – And Which One is Right for You

Meditation is a technique that is used to cultivate mindfulness. The practice of meditation alters one's state of mind, bringing an elevated sense of consciousness along with improving focus. Meditation is ancient, transcending throughout many different cultures and religions from all over the world. While meditation is most commonly associated with the Buddhist and Hindu religions, it is also practiced in Judaism, Christianity and Islam as well.

There are countless ways that people choose to meditate. However, almost all meditative practices fit into one of three categories, concentrative, mindfulness or guided meditation.

Concentrative meditation is concerned with achieving the highest state of being possible. As the name implies, here the emphasis is on complete and total concentration. Most of the time, the practitioners elect to place all of their focus upon their breathing, though others prefer to concentrate on the repetition of certain words of phrases which make up a mantra.

Mindfulness meditation is less concerned with concentrating on something specific and more geared around achieving a state of mindfulness. Here, the practitioner utilizes meditation to promote a greater awareness of the here and now. Mindful meditation places emphasis on being present in the moment and opening oneself to experiencing their surrounding with an open, non-judgmental mind. This form of meditation is particularly beneficial in alleviating stress along with anxiety and depression.

Guided meditation involves one or more people taking part in a meditation session that is verbally led by a trained practitioner. This teacher actually acts as a guide, providing you with auditory input that influences the act of meditation. Guided meditation usually happens in a face to face environment, yet it is also effective through recorded audio or even simply via reading a text. Guided meditation is very useful in helping someone resolve an issue through the meditative process. The guide helps to construct a meditative session that is tailored to the individual's particular need. For example, if the person meditating has been struggling with grief, the guide may gear the session in such a way that the person is led through a mental exercise in which they are able to release some of the pain and begin the process of letting go. Guided meditation is very successful in clinical practice, helping alleviate symptoms of anxiety and depression.

Hidden Benefits of Meditation You Never Knew About

Meditation can reduce levels of anxiety and stress

Regular participation in meditation can actually help us train our minds to experience less stress and anxiety. By utilizing what is called the relaxation technique, the practitioner combines concentrative and mindfulness meditation. The relaxation technique involves focusing upon and repeating a singular word in order to bring ourselves into the present moment. By repeating the word and focusing upon existing only in the here and now, the body achieves a sense of serenity and calm. If we practice the relaxation technique enough, it is easier to train our bodies to go into a relaxed state when we are faced with external stressors.

Meditation can increase levels of self-awareness

Many times, when we are faced with a stressful situation, our minds automatically revert to old habits and coping mechanisms. Rather than immediately responding with increased levels of stress and anxiety when a challenge presents itself, meditation helps us stop and honestly evaluate the situation. When we learn to take a moment and reflect before reacting emotionally to a problem, we find that we are able to take on that situation with greater wisdom and clarity. Regularly practicing meditation helps us increase self-awareness by helping us to stay in the present. Achieving this mindful state reminds us that we have dealt with difficult situations before, and survived to tell the tale.

Meditation is good for your health

Not only does meditating boost the immune system, it alleviates physical ailments that result from carrying too much stress and tension around. Thus, regular meditation can decrease blood pressure, help us sleep better and can even help us lose weight, as we tend to be more mindful as to what we are putting in our body.

Meditation improves our memory and helps us concentrate

The practice of meditation involves going within oneself and remaining still. This is easier said than done in the busy world that we live in. By regularly giving yourself time to simply sit and focus upon being in the moment, it becomes easier to focus upon the task at hand when dealing with our day to day tasks. The mounting to do list that greets us at the beginning of each day can seem overwhelming when we look at everything we need to get done. Yet, if we are able to break the list down into smaller steps and simply focus upon achieving one goal at a time, the process does not seem as daunting.

Meditation can help improve our relationships

Studies have shown that people who engage in regular meditation are naturally more empathetic. When we focus only upon getting through the day, it is easy to lose track of the fact that we are surrounded by others who's needs and desires are just as significant as our own. Meditation opens us up to a sense of universal consciousness, meaning that we become more aware of our place in the world as a whole rather than thinking of ourselves as a singular, lone entity. When we are able to pick up on the emotional needs of others and treat them as seriously as we would our own, a greater sense of understanding is achieved. A behavior that would normally spark irritation or anger, such as not feeling as though our significant other is listening to us, is instead treated as an opportunity to learn what that person is trying to tell us by their actions.

Some classrooms have begun to replace punishment with mindfulness. This means that an infraction that would normally land a student in detention instead results in time spent in mindfulness and meditation. These schools have found that they experience a dramatic decrease in problem behaviors, such as acting aggressively towards other students or refusing to focus upon the task at hand. Rather than focusing solely upon punishing the student, meditation instead gives the student the opportunity to relax, regroup and focus upon their own behavior and how it affects others.

Meditation can boost levels of creativity

Many writers, entertainers and artists find that they receive some of their best inspiration through the process of meditation. It provides us with a space to clear our minds of anything unimportant, thus allowing the inspirational juices to flow freely. Many people who regularly meditate actually create a sacred space inside their heads which they visit frequently. Within this space, we not only find increased levels of confidence and contentment, but also open ourselves us to receiving inspiration.

Meditation enhances spirituality

Whether or not you consider yourself religious, participating in meditation helps to put you in touch with a higher power. Spirituality involves getting in touch with our inner selves, and meditation helps us do this. By creating a quiet space in which we can simply be still, we are able to better focus our intentions and open ourselves to the subtle energies surrounding us.

Meditation can help combat negative behaviors

While meditation is something that anyone can do, it does take practice. Learning how to block out outside distractions and simply focus upon the moment is more difficult than it sounds, particularly if we have been raised to believe we must constantly be doing or accomplishing something. Meditation forces us to develop self-discipline. This self-disciple coupled with the cultivation of a safe, serene space inside our minds can be extremely helpful in combatting addictions or other self-destructive tendencies.

Meditation can decrease physical pain levels

We all suffer from physical discomfort from time to time. For most of us, we choose to just grin and bear it, ignoring the signs our bodies are giving us and pushing through with the day's tasks. Meditation not only helps us slow down and listen to the cues our body provides, it has also been shown to actually stimulate the areas of the brain which are responsible for numbing physical pain.

How to meditate, even if you've never done it before in your life...

While there are countless different approaches and methods for meditation that you can choose to learn from, the truth is that there is no singular right or wrong way to do it. Some people insist on constructing all sorts of formal rules and regulations around the practice, believing that you must engage in meditation first thing in the morning. Others think that there must be a certain kind of incense, music or other tools present to achieve the desired results. Meditation is a very personal process. If you get the best results first thing in the morning, then by all means, this is when you should meditate. Likewise, if having music playing softly in the background helps you, keep that music playing for as long as you'd like.

But what if you can't meditate early in the morning, because you need to get up and get your kids ready for school before you go to work? What is music playing in the background is a distraction, and burning incense doesn't do anything other than give you a headache?

The best meditative ritual for you to establish will be to figure out what works for you, and to do it. Don't worry if someone else says its wrong, or insists you should be doing it differently. Although there are no absolute rules when it comes to meditating, there are a few general guidelines to help you get started.

Step One: Remove yourself from any distractions you can

Finding a quiet place where you will be free from interruption is harder than you may think. Even if you manage to steal away for a few moments, there is still the phone going off constantly or a toddler calling your name just outside the door. No matter how much we may wish it to be different, life does not stop and start at our convenience. Thus, it is important to find a time and place for meditation that works for you. Even with the best laid plans, recognize that there will be times you are interrupted, and that is okay. The goal is to try to set yourself up for a distraction-free environment the best you can. Pick a time when you are alone in the house with at least fifteen or twenty minutes to spare. If there is no one else present that can demand your attention, the only one who can present a distraction is yourself.

This is where you need to prepare accordingly. Leave your phone in a different room, or if you insist on having it with you, turn it off or at the very least, silence it. With the exception of a true emergency, there is nothing that is going to happen in this time you are taking for yourself that can't wait for a response. Even better, after engaging in meditation, you will be better prepared to react to any situation with mindfulness rather than blind emotion. We all love our pets, but this is a time when it is probably better to close the door, as you don't want to reach a relaxed state only to have the cat jump into your lap or the dog lick your face!

If you live with other people where alone time is virtually impossible, don't be afraid to speak up for yourself. Tell your roommates that you need a little while by yourself, and ask them not to disturb you unless it is absolutely necessary. Explain the importance of what you are doing for yourself to your spouse and ask them to keep the children occupied so you have a moment to center yourself.

Step Two: Prepare your mind and body

Yes, you can meditate anytime, anywhere, as we will see later on. With that being said, there are certain things that you can do to ensure that your body and mind are in the best state possible to achieve mindfulness.

First of all, the importance of getting enough sleep cannot be overstated. Most people find that they function best when they get anywhere from seven to nine hours of sleep each night. Too little sleep can leave us with difficulty concentrating and an overall cranky disposition, while too much sleep is just as harmful, resulting in depression and lethargy. Strive your best to go to bed at a reasonable time and likewise, make the effort to get up and get going at a decent hour as well.

Second, it is best to only engage in meditation when you are not under the influence of alcohol or drugs. While it may seem as though having a few drinks or engaging in other recreational drug use would help with relaxation and expanding the mind, keep in mind that the goal of meditation is to achieve clarity and mindfulness. By definition, drugs and alcohol have an affect on our state of consciousness, making it ultimately harder to achieve the state of focus we are after.

Step Three: Get comfy

It is very hard to relax when you aren't comfortable. You want to be sure that you pick a space which has a soft, padded space for you to sit, whether it is a cushion, a specific mat or simply plush carpeting. Likewise, don't dress in anything that is constricting, as you want to be able to breathe freely and focus upon the moment, not how itchy your shirt is. Check the temperature to be sure it is what you like before you begin as well.

Some people have a specific room or area in their home that is dedicated solely to the purpose of meditation. They cultivate an environment of beauty and sacredness in this area, preparing it with only the things that bring them the greatest sense of joy. While it is certainly not realistic for everyone to have a meditation room, you do want to try to create a sacred space for yourself. This means clearing the area of any clutter and surrounding yourself with the things that make you happy, whether it be a bouquet of fresh flowers, an animal figuring or the joy of smelling your favorite candles burning. Get rid of anything that makes you feel anxious, sad or angry, at least for the purpose of while you're meditating.

Step Four: Have a seat

Sit in a position that is comfortable, and rest your hands so the palms are facing up. Some people prefer to lie down while they meditate, and this is fine, as long as you are able to not fall asleep!

Step Five: Breathe and focus

For the first few minutes, simply sit and breathe normally with your eyes closed. As your breath starts to fall into a rhythm, focus upon that rhythm and slowly start to breath deeper and slower. This will naturally help you begin to relax. Try to focus your mind only upon your breathing. If you start to get mentally sidetracked, just pull yourself back to thinking about your breath.

Step Six: Visualize

Meditation helps us all create our own special place that we can turn to in times of turmoil for guidance and wisdom. Oftentimes this area that lies within us gets gradually built up over time and with each session of meditation. If you are just beginning, once your body feels fully relaxed and you are focused only on your breathing, allow yourself to envision a space that speaks to you on a soul level. For some people, it is a sandy tropical beach or wooded forest while for others, it might be as simple as a room. Whatever mental setting makes you feel content and joyful is the one to develop as time goes on.

Some people elect to participate in guided meditation. This involves an outside source providing clues during the meditative process. This is a particularly good tool for those who are new to meditation, as it helps to develop visualization skills.

Chapter Four: 8 Exercises for Everyday Mindfulness You Can Do at Home...with no extra cost

Exercise One: Experience food on every level

Take a piece of your favorite fruit, whether it be an apple, banana, cherry, peach, mango or strawberry. The goal is to experience this fruit fully by focusing your senses. First, feel the fruit in your hands, whether with your eyes closed or open. Feel the texture of its skin – is it smooth or bumpy? Fuzzy or naked? Tough or soft? Second, take the fruit in with your eyes, observing every detail you can, from color to any blemishes that may exist. Third, smell the fruit and experience any memories you may have associated with that aroma. Finally, bite into the fruit and taste it fully. This is an exercise that can be done with almost any food, not only to help us have a greater enjoyment of each meal, but also to keep our brains focused on the immediate moment.

Exercise Two: Relax yourself bit by bit

Sit or lie down in a comfortable position. Begin by regulating your breathing, then focus on each part of your body individually, feeling it relax as you go along. For example, begin by focusing upon your toes and feeling each one relax before moving on to your ankles, foot, lower legs, upper legs, hips, etc before finally arriving at the top of the head. This helps us to hone our focus by forcing us to concentrate on one area of the body at a time while still relaxing the system as a whole.

Exercise Three: Take it all in

If you live in an area where the weather is permitting, dress yourself comfortably and head outside. Find an area you are naturally drawn to, and make yourself comfortable. Simply sit and be in the moment, taking in anything that you see. This could be anything from simply watching a cloud pass over the sun or leaves falling in the autumn wind to a squirrel gathering nuts or even a fellow wandered making their way by. The point is to sit in stillness and fully take in what is occurring around you without making judgments. Try to look at things only as they are, without reading anything else into it. If something in particular draws your focus, such as bird flitting from branch to branch, absorb yourself in the experience as much as you are able. This exercise helps us learn how to fully take on what is going on around us without harboring expectations and/or judgment.

Exercise Four: Train your thoughts

Our thoughts have an incredible impact upon our minds, and therefore, our experience of reality. The undeniable power of positive thinking has been long acknowledged by psychiatrists and scientists alike since Dr. Norman Vincent Peale released his book pf the same title in 1952. Following the simple rule of like attracts like, we understand that if we have negative expectations regarding a situation, we are far more likely to experience those same negative aspects than someone who greets the problem with an optimistic mindset.

This exercise helps us train our brains to replace negative thoughts with positive ones. It involves constant vigilance, meaning that we must actually think about what we are thinking. Anytime we catch ourselves thinking something negative, such as "I'll never be able to get that done," or "I can't do anything right," we immediately replace it with a positive, empowering thought. Instead of convincing ourselves that we won't ever be able to study enough to get a good grade on our final exam, we instead focus upon the steps we can take to ensure that we will do the absolute best that we can do. The longer we engage in this exercise, the easier it becomes, as our brains can actually re-wire themselves to think positively rather than negatively.

Exercise Five: Find your happy place

This is a simple, easy technique for cultivating mindfulness that can be done quickly and in nearly any environment. If you find yourself faced with a stressful or emotional situation, take a few minutes and try to calm yourself as best as you can. Once you are relaxed, close your eyes and recall one of the happiest memories you have. It can be a place you once visited, a person whose company you immensely enjoy or any other number of things, as long as it brings you an intense feeling of joy and contentment. Picture this favorite place, thing or person in your head as clearly as you can, soaking in all of the positive energy the vision supplies you with. Then simply open your eyes and go about your day with a renewed focus and energy.

Exercise Six: Work with a guide

As people get into the regular process of meditation, many find that they establish a connection with some sort of internal guide along the way. This guide can appear in many different forms, although most commonly, it is another person or some sort of animal. If the idea of working with a spirit guide appeals to you, try the following exercise.

Once your breathing is regulated and you are fully relaxed, ask your guide to appear to you in your minds eye. Do not try to force anything, and do not pass any kind of judgment on any visual input you may receive. Simply note what happens, and keep practicing this technique for as long as you need to before you are able to establish a rapport with your guide.

Exercise Seven: Surround yourself with light

This is a quick, easy exercise that can be done nearly anytime and in anyplace. If you should find yourself feeling overwhelmed, anxious or stressed out, find a quiet place you can escape to for a minute. This might mean retreating to the bathroom at work, or shutting yourself in a room at home. Once you are alone, shut your eyes, take a few deep breaths and visualize a soft blue light surrounding you. See this vision as clearly as you can in your mind's eye, and as you watch the light envelop you, release whatever tension it is you are carrying. Allow this light to encircle you, bringing comfort and serenity. As you get ready to end the session, visualize yourself drawing the light into yourself. When you open your eyes, you will feel a dramatic increase in contentment and peace.

Exercise Eight: Stress in, stress out

This is a good way to take five minutes out of your day to release any negative emotions and regain a state of mindfulness. Find a comfortable spot to sit for a moment, and focus on your breathing. Once your breathing has become regular and deep and you are feeling relaxed, begin to visualize. Picture any stress, sadness, anger or other negative emotion inside of you as a grey smoke that leaves your body every time your exhale. As you breathe in picture a brilliant white light swirling around you and enter your body. This white light collects inside of you and builds up until your whole body is glowing and sparkling, as each bit of grey inside of you is expelled. Once your entire body is filled with light, slowly picture that light condensing itself in your center, between where your heart and hips are. As this light grows smaller, see it become concentrated into a pure ball of positive energy. Hold this image for a few breaths, and then slowly count to ten to re-center yourself.

www.ingramcontent.com/pod-product-compliance
Lightning Source LLC
Chambersburg PA
CBHW071034080526
44587CB00015B/2617